DATE:

....

FROM:

....

PRESENTED TO:

....

© 2017 TOYIN MOORE

First published by Toyin Moore

ISBN: 978-1-9997272-7-7

Because of the dynamic nature of the Internet, any web addresses or links contained in this book may have changed since publication and may no longer be valid.

I DID A VERY BAD THING

WHAT PEOPLE ARE SAYING

Wow! Wow!! Wow!!! Ty Moore has done an amazing work with her book,   I did a bad think. It's not every day you come across a book as real and down to earth as this very particular book I HAVE DONE A BAD THING. In our world, today whereby so many people are leaving under the weight of their past mistakes especially women, this book then is a breath of fresh air. I believe this book is going to bless you tremendously and help you to know that irrespective of your past mistakes, God still loves you abundantly. I personally love this book and I will like to recommend this book to everyone. Especially those who are still struggling to forgive themselves for their past mistake and are having a difficult time believing that God still lives them irrespective of their shortcomings. Thank you so much Ty for the wonderful work you did with this book and the real-life story used to be able to connect with your readers perfectly. God, bless you greatly. May God s blesses rest upon you all as you read this book.

DR. Bien Sufficient.
President,
Kingdom Lifestyle Movement (KLM)

WHAT PEOPLE ARE SAYING

An extremely encouraging book ... at times we do not chose what happens to us however life happens; memories are created and remind us in each day of what paths we have walked. In some cases, it makes others weak and for some it makes them stronger ... In reading Ty Moore's book I was filled with many emotions; *pain, sadness, fear, need and despair*; it is however most important to note that the sentiments I was left with were those of **victory, strength**, a new way of understanding and acceptance that though life happens it does so to strengthen us and shape us to be the giants we ultimately become. I am certain that anyone that reads this book will be encouraged that painful tears will always turn into tears of joy, for The Lord God our Creator created us in his image for a worthwhile purpose. Well done to you Ty Moore; your bravery attitude will no doubt empower someone else. May God continue to bless you.

Lady Waynett Peters
CEO & Founder of
The Extraordinary Achievers
& Dappers and Divas

DEDICATION

This is to women, who despite their CRIP- PLING AND DEBILI-TATING pasts, especially every woman who has had a CRIMSON PAST and questioned her ever having a good FU- TURE, yet having fought and clung on TENA- CIOUSLY TO TRUTH, LOVE AND FAITH knowing that GOD does exist and will ULTIMATELY be GOOD TO US HIS CHILDREN.

FOREWARD

It is a joy and a privilege for me to get to know TY Moore. The story of our acquaintance is well documented in this book as you read through you will get that information for yourself. The book you are holding in your hand is a book that will bring you to tears and to laughter, to brokenness and to ecstasy such is the depth of feelings and emotions that are well expressed and articulated in this book. The stories in this book will not leave you indifferent, get ready to change. This book will pour into you an unmeasurable dose of energy and adrenaline such as you will like to begin to do something with your life. TY has decided to offer herself literally on the altar of sacrifice so that the fire of revival will burn deep in your heart. Through her life story and experience, she is convincingly appealing to all of us to live the best life that God has sent us here for. The results that she has been able to achieve since she woke from her slumber in less than a year has been mind- blowing. This gives all of us the confidence and the faith to know that if TY could turn all negativity in her life to such a huge springboard for success then so can anyone of us. I therefore want to tell everyone that is holding this book to begin to congratulate him or herself. This is your chance to start a new life, this book is God s gift to you. Congratulations and Enjoy. Big thanks to TY, for paying the price to provide this book to the world to read.

DR. Sunday Adelaja

FORWARD

Reading this book, I see It takes a healed soul to open and share her life experience in detail for others to learn, be encouraged and be set free from the bondage of the enemy and spirit of guilt. I love the Nuggets at the end of each chapter. It is indeed wisdom nuggets and it sticks with you even after you must have dropped the book.

Holding and reading this book will make you see that all that you have gone through in life that you call limitations are, things that are there to make you fulfil your destiny. Once abused but later go out to reach out to the abused shows you have been healed.

Whatever you have gone through and come out of, you are qualified to go and deliver others in the similar situations, problems or challenges. You do not need to wait, you earned that experience for a purpose. Ty Moore book should be termed 'a systematic way of deliverance' for so many singles and married out there. Thanks Ty Moore for this *Life Experience Transforming book*.

Yours in His Vineyard
Kemi Onadipe
MMMW UK

This is a thought provoking booklIt is the story of a woman's life journey from naivety to maturity (Spiritual and psychological) A journey of discovery in God.The importance of having a personal relationship with Christ cannot be over emphasised. I reccomend this book for young ladies.

Mrs Stella Mopelola Oluyede

PREFACE

Do you know what it feels like to realize that you have been alive for a few decades and yet not been living. To suddenly see that one has been existing and merely getting by instead of experiencing life in all its fullness as is intended by God for every single human being on the earth, Jew, Greek Hindu or Muslim. It was like the great awakening of the living dead. That was the feeling I had when I met Dr Sunday Adelaja, you see I was in some sort of plateau. I am a firm believer in the Lord Jesus Christ and I am also a faithful Church goer and have been going to church from my teen age. However, my whole perception on Christianity took an immense paradigm shift on realizing I had not been living up to my full potential.

Don't get me wrong I would say I have had my fair share of challenges and victories, in fact some would look at me as a very successful person, seeing where I started and how far God had brought me. I was introduced to Dr Sunday with the sole aim of Producing a feature film, a Bio film about the life and story of Sunday Adelaja. How was I to know that so much more lay within me. My world literally sky rocketed, in a way I did not know I was capable of, in taking strides that were ginormous, almost dreamlike.

I became embolden after reading some of his books and listening to testimonies by people who had transited from been the dregs of society into leaders in their com- munities and even becoming part of people who influenced policy in their countries. Former drug addicts turned to community leaders, destitute single parents (ladies) going back to school and getting Doctorates and so forth. One thing stood out about these people, they took the bad, ugly sad and unfortunate incidents in their lives and used it as fuel to turn their lives around. They also were not ashamed to acknowledge their sordid past but rather used it in challenging and encouraging others in that same situation to come out and be better. If they could, surely those still in these vices can as well. These people and the teachings from Dr Sunday Adelaja, gave me the courage to confront something I had hidden away in my past for over 20 years. I was ashamed and thought to speak of it would be damaging to me. What would people say syndrome. Also for the first time I realized that my shame and pain can be used to liberate other people who may also be imprisoned by these things. I then set out to speak about my past, my failures, my experiences and how I got healed. I started my own Live Face Book Broadcast called TY S DIARIES and this book is an of shoot of that broadcast. Knowing this great man has further engrafted in my heart the notion that we are loved by God and each have a definite assignment here on earth, our responsibility is to discover who we are and why we are here on earth. Its only when we know this that we can live a truly fulfilling life.

Content	Page

Content   Page

I DID A VERY BAD THING

INTRODUCTION :

A Prodigal Mother A modern story for modern times. I am telling this story for many reasons, I feel that I have been telling this story before through my work in film but that there is still a part of me that is hiding behind the stories that I tell. I made a video that brought this home to me and after thinking about it and the impact that it had upon me I feel that it is time for me to step up and be honest in the hope that it will help others who have experienced the same pain that I have carried all these years. It isn't easy for a black woman raised in the arms of the Lord and the love of the Church to relate this story as I carried the shame and the guilt for so long, fearful of what others would say and think and how I would be judged. Yet I have come to realize over time that it is only God s judgement that I needed to be concerned with, I am human and therefore imperfect. God gives us all choices and that there are times when we are in dark places that we feel the light of the Lord cannot reach us and we get lost because we cannot see him. I made a choice that has haunted me when I was in this dark place but what I didn't realize was that this was what needed to happen to make me the person that I am today. It brought me nearer to God and allowed me to truly know the power of His forgiveness and truly appreciate all that I have now far more than if it had never happened. I have come to realize that as human beings we can be selfish yet the Lord asks us to be more than this, to be greater than what we are.

> Many times, when we go for interventions one of the things people are advised to do is talk about it. AM TALKING ABOUT IT.

To do this I must come out of my comfort zone, the safe place where you only show what you feel is the acceptable or appropriate face. I need to be honest with the Lord and myself. I realized that I should bring out all the things I had hidden and tell all the experiences I had gone through. No matter how sordid, ugly or un- acceptable to the norm. To help someone else, to free somebody who may be going through the same thing and to prevent others from falling into the same pits. This would mean dying to self-esteem, public opinion, church expectation and so on and so forth. It is this that has pushed me to tell my story, to be selfless and honest with those around me so that I can hope to give something back to those who might find themselves in the same position that I was in and let them know that the Lord still loves them even if they don t. I also realize that for me to not just be healed of my pains and hurt but to be made whole, I should pour out all. Healing sometimes takes time and is in phases, sometimes it can be days, months or even years, especially for psychological traumas. They are wounds not visible and so may not get treated as effectively as the physical visible wounds.

But our God is a healing God, His blood shed on Calvary over 2 thousand years ago can flow to the lowest valley into the crevices of our lives and experiences, it can reach to the highest mountains and it can calm the strongest of storms in our mind, if we only let Him.

Many times, when we go for interventions one of the things people are advised to do is talk about it. AM TALKING ABOUT IT.

GOD SAID YOU ARE MY WIFE

1. GOD SAID YOU ARE MY WIFE

> You are not condemned for your sins but for the sin of rejecting the only begot- ten of God, receive Him today and be saved you and your whole household

Most times people assume that sin is out there in the world, from the bad children of the Devil Because surely a born-again child of God was a saint or is supposed to be a saint and if tempted the temptation must be from the Devils outside ERRR INFORMA- TION ALERT . we all have our own personal demons. We have our struggles, our hang-ups, our unresolved issues, our habits that have been formed for years and need to be over hauled and deliberately challenged and changed. (Romans 12:1-2). Not to mention erroneous teachings, and selfish inordinate desires that we cover up so perfectly under the guise of na Devil cause am or people of the world (awon Aiye). My brothers and I, full of zeal for God and determined to save the world, embarked on evangelism every day . We lived in the Mafoluku area of Lagos in Nigeria. I was the ring leader and only female, the other 2 were my younger brothers Daniel and Johnson. Both have gone on to become great men of God in their different spheres, Johnson went to Mali and then eventually settled in France, His life is one absolutely trail blazing testimony. That is a story for another day. Daniel, on the other hand, started off as a full missionary, going to the Gambia s, Sierra Leone, eventually is established in media related work and is based in West Africa These two were my co-gangsters for God, occasionally we would have one or 2 others join in the group. I had read in the book of Mark 16;15.

Go ye into the world and preach the gospel in my name heal the sick, cast out Demons We went out looking for who to get saved and noticed that in our area, that there were these women who had twins and for some reason they would seat on a stool with the twin children on the pedestrian bridge or bus stops begging for alms.

I just was heartbroken every time I go past these people, but they are Yoruba speaking people. Now I could understand Yoruba but was not very strong in speaking it. This is because my mum hails from Ogun state in Nigeria, a Yoruba speaking people but she had married my Dad a man from Delta State when she was very young and so was more of a Delta woman than Yoruba, to add to this, English was our first language at home. I feel very sad about that now.

Seeing then that I could not really engage these people much in Yoruba, we decided to get their attention via gifts, so I took baby stuff from home and from friends. We took nice baby shawls, clothes etc. We then we used our small konkolo widow s mite and bought Ogi (This is Pap, a common food that Africans feed to babies), we bought the very healthy one made from millet known as Ogi baba Armed with our best as teen-agers we then went to these women and did our best telling them about Jesus and how he can save us from our sins, we held spontaneous crusades under the bridge at this very big bus stop known as OSHODI, and people would gather and we would preach, shout, teach, pray, cast out demons, God help you if we came across you, you had to hear about Jesus because the world would soon come to an end as the Lord was coming soon. Oh, such zeal.

Having exhausted all the known Bus stops near us we decided to take it further and would join big public buses called Molue where sometimes it's so full we would have to stand and then we would belt out in our loudest voice telling people to give their lives to Christ, BE BORN AGAIN FOR GOD SO LOVED THE WORLD THAT HE GAVE HIS ONLY BEGOTTEN SON, you are not condemned for your sins but for the sin of rejecting the only begotten of God, receive Him today and be saved you and your whole household", not just that, we would then ask for the sick to step up or lift their hands and we would pray commanding sicknesses out, many testified of been healed.

Why am I telling us all these? I want to give us a back ground of the kind of girl I was and the kind of man it was I got pregnant for. You see on one of these evangelism waka we met a young man! Meanwhile people just loved to listen to us because we were speaking foneh. You see we were private school trained children taught to speak impeccable queens English, and preaching to folks Oshodi, Agege, Orile in Lagos State. These are areas where the not so posh people live, so we were more like a tourist attraction, but because we were so on fire and sincere God been faithful to his word confirmed our words with signs following always. One day we encountered a young man on one of our trips. We had asked those who wanted to be born-again and who also wanted the baptism in the Holy spirit to step out with us at the stop we came out on, and we were praying for some people when this young man (I will call him John) stepped out.

He prayed with us for these folks, I mean he was on fire, real geem geem, (meaning hot Christian) He would pray for the sick and people would get healed, he had the gift of healing and he had such charisma and power of persuasion. From that day, he introduced himself as a young pastor in training and that he would like to ac- company us on the days we wanted to go out on evangelism. He soon was introduced to my friends and my brothers everyone looked at him in awe and respect as he seemed to demonstrate so much boldness and power of God.

However, he was from a very rough background and a different part of the world from ours if you get my gist. We attended different schools of faith, I was of the Kenneth Hagin and Christ Chapel International Church, we were the   yuppie   Christians, Charismatic Americana type and he was the Fire and brimstone 'all the witches must die now' type of back- ground. All my friends loved him and would swoon over him, he also introduced us to his circle of friends, a little bit rough around the edges but we were all lovers of Jesus Christ, one big happy family. My father, as I clearly re- member did not really like him, my Dad once saw him come to our house early in the morning to ask after me, he always had this big Dake's Annotated bible that he carried with Him. My Dad, bless him, told him off and asked him to go get a job instead of coming to young ladies' home carrying a big bible early in the morning.

> We attended different schools of faith, I was of the Kenneth Hagin and Christ Chapel International Church, we were the yuppie Christians, Charismatic Americana type and he was the Fire and brimstone 'all the witches must die now' type of back- ground.

I DID A VERY BAD THING

One day he told me that GOD said I WAS HIS WIFE!! Wow!! Imagine. I was confused. I mean, I was not at all interested in marrying him or anyone else for that matter. Marriage was just not some- thing I was entertaining at that time. Mr John or Hot pastor John and I had nothing in common, we spoke very different languages, for example, he believed that he would be very rich cause he is so anointed he will have a big church and his congregants will buy him big cars houses and he would work so many miracles people would just be blessing him. I on the other hand believed that you should have a job, earn a living and don t live off people.

I hated the very concept of being a leech. We would argue endlessly over this and this was the man God said was to be my husband?!, Aaah!!! not to mention that every time he spoke I could not stand his vocabulary or mannerism, even when he ate he had such awful table manners. These were things I felt were tolerable as a 'brother' but as a husband, no way! I was confused. How can God do this to me. You see I believed he was an oracle of God. If he said God told him then it was true. I never thought to question him at all. I told my friends and tried to express my concerns, but every one of them were in favor of my marrying him.

It was in their eyes a match made in heaven. I was told how the will of God was not always pleasurable, but our lives were meant to be a living sacrifice.

Even if we don t like it we should submit to God's Will because God knows best and to disobey God was to be rebellious. Rebellion was as the spirit of witchcraft Everyone including my brothers were all rooting

21   *I DID A VERY BAD THING*

for him, so   like a sheep led to the slaughter and opened not his mouth, not my will Lord but yours be done, I consented. Like play like play, my mum was told, he told his folks, my pastor was told. (he was one of my senior pastors new protege so everything seemed perfect). But I was dying slowly, my once bubbly self was becoming more and more morose, but I kept up appearances, after all, Jesus suffered the cross for the joy that was before Him. Shortly after this he started taking me on his preaching engagements.

I was his 'trophy wife' to be, the Phonetics speaking worship leader, from an international church, going to be First Lady, some people even had the effrontery to be calling me MAMMA (eg- bami)I was just so young and I simply hated all the fuss. Now he had started trying to touch me inappropriately, you know, making attempts to kiss me, fondle me but I would fob it off, person wey I nor even like sef, so it probably made it easy for me to claim holiness ..I honestly cannot say that it was holiness that was making me refuse it was more of simply being turned off, period. I didn't like the man. He then started mounting pressure, I mean he would shed tears, and beg me to show him that I love him, that he was not loved as a child and he suffered maltreatments, the guy worked me up emotionally using any kind of blackmail to evoke some sympathetic hug and stuff and 'Mumu' that I was, I would hug him and feel sorry for him, but I honestly was not feeling it, however I was just going along.

RAPE

1. RAPE

> It was like an insane animal, he tore off the underwear and I was being raped by my man of God!

One day we went on a weekend preaching assignment. We set off in the morning and it was such a long journey. When we got to this place eventually, after we had taken 2 boat rides into some interior part of town, someplace I had never been before. It was a small town/community or village. They had some holiday cabins built for Europeans on holiday as most of this coastline small communities often did to generate income. The rest of the accommodations were very poor ramshackle houses where most of the indigenes resided. I noticed that almost every house had a wooden bowl filled with food particles, blood stains and dripping with palm oil in front of them. This indicates food offered as sacrifice to Idols, it was an obviously idolatrous people. We arrived late evening and you can imagine the state of my mind, alone with this my powerful evangelist to be husband, with strangers in a voo-doo isolated village, out of civilization plus they had no electricity, just lamps and some generators to generate light for a while. I could never forget that experience. Soon it was night we were shown to where we would be for the night.

We were their esteemed guests so they offered us their humble best. It was basically one of the make-shift cabin resorts for white holiday makers. It consisted of a room, enclosed toilet and shower and that was it! This I was told was where we both were staying for the night. I was alarmed that we were going to sleep on the same bed? Alone, together, unmarried? Hello???

As soon as the people left he calmly said   these are poor people, they cannot even pay money for the preaching", he further said that they most likely would pay with their catch of the day. (Fishing community) He explained how in the past they would pay by giving him a bag of smoked fish and sometimes when they have had a very good catch they would include lots of smoked prawns as well. I should please not ask for anything more as this was their best accommodation. We should sleep as the next day was Sunday and we were speaking as Guest ministers at the big convention for these poor folks. We were the visiting preachers, mighty man and woman of God come to preach good news. Worn out from the everlasting journey, I soon fell asleep after taking my bath. Bone tired and exhausted I did not know when this my Evangelist man of God and soon to be husband started undressing me. I felt someone tugging at my underwear on top of me!

Then ensued a mother of all struggles, I was already at a disadvantage, exhausted, vulnerable, and barely awake, he pinned me down and was like a beast, I was crying, begging, "please don t do this, please stop I beg you, what are you doing??! Please". H was like an insane animal, he tore off the underwear and I was being raped by my man of God! My fiancé, a strange room, in an isolated town among strangers, alone and far from home and everyone, I was being taking advantage of by the only person who was supposed to be my cover and protection. I eventually pushed him off. He had become so consumed with whatever he was doing and was not holding me down as strongly as before. I was sobbing and he was trying to get back on saying I should please let him finish, that he was almost there...

I don t know how to explain this, how does one even begin to articulate the myriad of emotions, confusion, fear, betrayal- waves of never ceasing emotions? I simply have no words to even qualify this experience, the word abuse seems simply inadequate to express all that was done to me that day. Trust shattered, faith questioned, weird mixed sense of guilt, perhaps I am somewhat responsible for this, feeling robbed, assaulted, broken, and broken, just broken.

Something got taken from me that day. Irreplaceable damage that seemed irreparable. I was further stunned by the fact that he was angry and sulking, because I did not let him   finish   He then sim- ply rolled over and fell asleep. I stayed awake and just too scared to sleep again, I kept dozing and jerking up in fright till morning. I remember how he smelled. I could smell him and for many months probably years that smell was there lingering in my memory. Folks rape is by far one of the vilest things that can be done to any- one. The effects are far reaching, way beyond just the physical hurt itself. I was to find out later in life, that this heinous act had a negative effect on my future relationships with men and with the very act of love making or sexual intercourse. The next morning, he got dressed and simply acted as though nothing had happened. I got dressed too, but my world had been shattered. I felt so alone yet surrounded by people, I was in auto drive, somehow, we made it to church, to add insult upon injury he got on the pulpit and said Please welcome my queen, my this, my that, as she leads us in God s presence before I start preaching.

I was so terrified and confused, I was angry and scared, we had done this evil thing and this man was asking me to climb on Gods pulpit, I thought

> The next morning, he got dressed and simply acted as though nothing had happened. I got dressed too, but my world had been shattered.

I DID A VERY BAD THING

surely today I will meet Ananias and Sapphira. Oh, Lord would this nightmare ever end? I was shaking and trying not to break down I was all teary and stuttering and like a robot but I took the microphone because people had gathered from nearby villages or town. The venue was packed all the way to the outside. They brought the sick, the lame and the demon possessed in this highly voodoo infested village.

I was simply at the mercy of God, so in my heart I cried out to my Father and our Present Help, the Holy Spirit, asking that they please not strike me dead for climbing the pulpit for I had sinned. You see, I saw myself as the sinner not as a victim. I felt absolutely lost and confused, almost running mad and yet had to put on a calm exterior. I'll always remember the song I sang, not because of the lyrics but because of the whole unforgettable experience;

Iba re Jesu o
Iba re Omoh Olorun
Eleru niyn mo juba re

Oma seun

and it was even more shocking how Gods prescience filled every- where. Our God is a very merciful God, His ways are unsearchable. People were lifting hands I was just crying because my world was over and I was before my king so if there was anyone to help me it was Him or no one else. Then this man got up and started preaching like he was not the beast of the night before, and the miracles began. Heeeeeey!!

I remember a woman with a still baby whom doctors we were told had asked to come for evacuation because baby was dead in her womb came, John prayed and laid hands, immediately the baby started kicking violently, it was surreal. Truly the gifts and calling of God are without repentance. Does this now mean that it's okay to commit heinous crimes because the miracles still happen? Oh no! I later learned as I matured in God that there is a day for reckoning, for Jesus himself said on that day despite the great works some attest to, He Christ will say to them;

"Get thee away from me, for I know you not, you worker of iniquity". A woman of God called Christine Moore once taught us about the priests of God who can minister to God's people but may not come into God's presence. May we never choose to be people pleasers above our one on one relationship with God.

NUGGETS
1. Even the devil wears collar. Just because he claims he is a man of God does not mean he is.
2. Do not under any circumstance share a bed with a man other than your husband except of unavoidable situations like Natural Disasters such as Earthquakes etc. If you must make sure you understand the parameters of that relationship.

THE BREAK-UP

2. THE BREAK-UP

> Why would I break the engagement so close to the wedding?

I cannot remember the journey back home but something was defi- nitely broken that day. When I got home I told him it was over, I did not ever want to see him again, he was to leave me alone. He cried begged said it was all caused by 'you know who?' "the Devil". He then started trying the familiar blackmail line, saying "God said you are my wife, and You cannot be disobedient to God." I decided then that if this decision is what will bring a quarrel between God and I, then so be it. Sorry God, I will not marry this man and since that would be against Your Will, You and I are probably done. I saw myself as walking against God, so I felt as though I was no longer under the protection of God. This meant that I could die, or fall sick, or any terrible thing could happen to me because of my sin of disobedience. The man of God had said "God said", and I was rebelling against that so I am doomed.

These were the type of messages we were taught back then and he John, kept telling me how disastrous things would befall me for disobeying the counsel of God. I stopped eating, I lost my appetite. I used to love to sing and worship God but I felt God probably does not want to hear me now, so I stopped singing praises or worship. I used to like to pray and tell God everything but now I was a sinner and no sinners can see God or be friends with God, so no praying. Cut off from my primary source of joy, hope and strength, I started to deteriorate. I stopped taking care of my appearance, I lost a desire for life. I was so unhappy and worried, my hair started falling out from the sheer stress. I had begun to lose weight, since I was not eating, and I was not interacting with anyone.

I DID A VERY BAD THING

My friends all got mad at me. Why would I break the engagement so close to the wedding? Dates had been fixed, I told the church the wedding was off, told my folks the wedding was off. My mother was sad and wanted me to reconsider. John was pressurizing because he went begging everyone to beg me, but no one knew why I broke it off and I was not telling. One day my late mum came to my room early morning crying and begging me to please not disgrace her and the family. They had picked ASO EBI (uniform cloth for guests and family) She had bought the cow the rice, all invites had been sent out and all expenses made already. How can I do this, she said.

She will be the laughing stock of her friends. I was her first daughter, she had done weddings for all her friends and our family people, now that it was her turn, why was this happening. She began begging me to please not bring shame on her head and on our family. The pressure was quite severe. I felt so alone. This was my mother and yet I could not bring myself to tell her. I was so ashamed and I also did not know how to tell her that   the man of God   had done this thing. Nor could I tell my friends or siblings. This was the   Man of God   they all were in awe of him, he was pious, anointed and from God. How could I even begin to say what he had done to me. Maybe I tempted him or maybe the devil made him do it, I was a mental wreck.

Instead of divulging what happened I simply asked my mum who was more important to her, Him or Me. I then asked if she wanted my happiness in life, but to marry him would be to condemn me to a life of unhappiness. I then started weeping, she asked me what was the problem I told her that all I know is that if I married him I would be very unhappy for the rest of my life.

My Mum, bless her soul even though shattered by this yet she loved me and wanted me to be happy, it must have looked confusing to her seeing I was losing weight, unhappy, and I was not exactly giving any coherent explanations. But Mummy chose to take me at my word that it was best to cancel the wedding. Thank God for a true mother s love who's bottom line looks out for her daughter first. Looking back, I wish I had told her what happened, maybe I may not have had to carry so many years of anguish, but that is what religion does to you, you don t think rationally anymore. Not to forget the shame and stigma of Rape. It's like a big stain and society does not look favourably on the raped woman. I was determined to not have anything to do with him. My relation- ship with my closest friends and church family was estranged. My relationship with my own family was estranged.

To make a bad situation worse I suddenly realized that I was pregnant!! What! How is that even possible? is it possible for one to get pregnant when the man did not exactly fully ejaculate? What a cruel twist. Aah! I was later told that while having sex men can sometimes release and it takes just one tiny microscopic sperm to impregnate a woman. Why or why me? Everything was dark, I started losing more weight, my hair was still falling out, I was mentally unbalanced, Losing my mind under the weight of my trauma. I stopped going to church in my heart, I was doing the motions but I was far away, pretty soon I stopped attending church physically. My business or job suffered, I was a big mess. In spites of all this, this man did not stop the harassment.

He now took it a notch higher by making threats, boasting about how anointed he was, and that he will call down thunder from heaven to strike me, he will send Angels to harm me. He made all sorts of threats it was now an unbelievable open war! I stood my ground and told him I was prepared to die but there was no way would I marry him. He could call down all the army of heaven for all I care.

Besides God and I were no longer talking so if God was not pleased with me, am sorry but am not going to marry him. I was so ignorant, I did not realize he was a fraud and that God was never part of this. I became very hostile to him and forbad him to come to my house. This was the final break up. I then went to see a doctor who was not a Christian, informed him about the pregnancy and requested an abortion. He refused to do the abortion for me, even though he was an experienced gynaecologist.

He was upset because he had asked me to use contraceptives but I refused claiming that since I was a child of God we don t have sex before marriage and therefore did not need to be put on the pill or use the 'coil', now here I was, this holy born again sister with an unwanted pregnancy. It was a very humiliating experience for me, so I went to the next available recommended Doctor who I knew I could not really vouch for. Some quack maybe with no track record, knowing this was very dangerous and could have costly implications but I was desperate.

I DID A VERY BAD THING

I could just not bring myself to having this child. I was bitter, afraid and in a very dark place, I believed that it was of no use even trying to go back to God or church since I had refused God's Will for my life. I was now on my own, having to make decisions by myself. That was how I found myself on that cold table with strangers ripping out my unborn child, alone and unable to cry out for help.

NUGGETS
1. Always follow your heart or conscience
2. Just because everyone says it's okay does not mean it's okay.

THE SCRATCHING SOUND

3. THE SCRATCHING SOUND

It all started inside my head, a scratching sound deep inside me, haunting me, it took so long for me to be able to not to hear it. I was a born again Christian, though estranged from God, I knew what I was doing was wrong, the conflict that I felt inside was a personal hell that I contained inside me and couldn't let out to anyone. I had been saved yet, I felt that I couldn't save myself. Thinking back now because of the shame I was feeling I couldn't t speak to anyone about it, it was if there were no options for me, only those that were unacceptable. Some people call this procedure with the clinical medical term, an evacuation, others call it what it is, an abortion.

I still find that word so difficult to speak, to me, I was literally killing my child, this is not an easy experience to go through and it is something that you can't forget. I was also aware that I was putting my life at risk. I was a teenage girl, like so many young women are when this happens, I was so scared and ashamed, I told no one, not my friends, not my Church and not my mother. It was the loneliest, isolating and frightening experience I have ever had. I remember the procedure like it was yesterday, I lay there on the cold clinical bed surrounded by strangers. I had been sitting in the reception area with other people before been called in. Some were young girls like me, and some were older girls.

The young ones looked scared and nervous mostly seating with a boyfriend or a friend. The older ones looked distant and aloof, like they were not there. As they prepared to put me under the anaesthetic I remember thinking that I may never wake from this.

> Some people call this procedure with the clinical medical term, an evacuation, others call it what it is, an abortion.

Part of me felt that I didn't deserve to wake up, but at the same time I didn't want to die, I wanted the chance to be able to prove to God that I could be better, that I could redeem myself in the eyes of the Lord. I prayed to God in my head, I could feel the tears running down my face in shame and fear, just me and God in that room as I prayed to him. I prayed God, I know that I am about to do a very bad thing, but please, don t let me die here, I give you back my soul for you to cleanse and make whole. I felt like I was in a dark tunnel and there was a voice that was saying to me that you might never come out of here again.

As they administered the injection and I felt the coldness of it going through my veins I prayed to God begging him to have mercy and save me, to show me the light that I may find him from this dark place. I could feel the fear gripping me inside as if death was going to take me and I went under. When I came to, I opened my eyes to see blood, so much blood everywhere, I looked at the nurses' eyes and could see their panic. The fear inside me, the doctors looked at me as if trying to be brave, I felt so helpless. Then they brought a bowl to me, inside this bowl was what remained of my child, so that I could see with my own eyes what I had done and said it's done, we have done the procedure.

This is an image that never leaves my mind, when I think about it now, I still feel the ultimate shame. Times were very different then. Society was not as accommodating then as it is now.

Harsh and severe consequences were meted out to the girl while the man often got away scot free. I can't tell you how shocking it was to see what I saw or how deeply that still affects me. This private clinic moved like a conveyer belt, they cleaned me up, gave me some tablets and shoved me out the door so they could at- tend to the long waiting line of un expectant young mothers. No one can prepare you for the effects of this operation, not only emotionally but also physically. There was no recovery time, it was almost as if they felt you deserved the pain you were going through. I remember trying to walk out of the clinic, I could barely stand up straight, I hobbled out bent over the pain inside me was excruciating, the tablets they gave me did nothing for the pain.

I had never felt so alone in my life, that no one would understand or want to know me if they knew what I had done, I cried and I prayed to God with my shame and guilt to not let me die, to please allow me to live, that I might find him again. I hailed a cab and huddled in the back seat gave the destination to the driver. He kept looking at me through the rear mirror and I kept averting his gaze. I'm sure he was wondering what was wrong with me but also not prying.

By the time, I got off I was a proper wreck, I had started shivering and my body temperature was running high. When I got home I went straight to my room, I didn't tell anyone, I couldn't tell anyone, I could only tell God, God was the only one I could speak to. The fever got worse and since I knew what I had just done I could not ask for help of any one so as not to risk exposure. I prayed to Him to spare my life. Thank God, He kept my secret and my life, God allowed me to live. That there was a reason that I could remain on this earth through his grace regardless of what sin I had done.

THE VISIT

One day a Minister of God and his wife came visiting the country. The year before I had served them when they visited from America. Unknown to me they had been praying for me, God had placed a burden in their heart for me. He later explained that they had a picture of me on their mantle place back in America, it was one of those photos taken when we were all together. He said God impressed on their heart to pray for me, that the burden would not lift, and that for months he and his wife had been interceding for me. Oh, this brings tears to my eyes, what a faithful God we serve, what a loving father, never leaving nor forsaking, a friend who sticks up for us always, wonderful Holy Spirit our Advocate and intercessor.

The visiting American minister insisted that I come with him to their hotel room, he claimed that his wife has instructed him not to return to their hotel without me. Would I please come and say hello to her so he will not get into trouble? I said I would come the next day. He said some other things I cannot remember and left. The next day I went to visit them. His wife asked me to stay for dinner they very gently encouraged me to come spend some time with them and even though it was not the norm at all for us to stay in their hotel with them they insisted I hang around them.

Everyday this couple were just loving on me and one day alone with his wife I told her everything that had happened to me. They were the ones God used to restore me and explain that God will not force his will on us and that If God could speak to the Evangelist he sure could speak to me.

> Every day I prayed to God thanking him for his blessing of sparing my life and praying that he would guide me to make me worthy of his love again.

They urged me to stay with them and like parents looked after me, financially emotionally and spiritually. There was another visiting minister with them, a lady in her late 20s and she had just gotten out of a bad abusive marriage, she asked me to stay in her room with her and shared her whole traumatic experience and how God healed and restored her and she is still a minister for God. They told me a broken engagement is far better than a broken marriage or a broken life. WOW! I was totally set free, so I did not have to stay in an abusive relationship to please God, who knew?? What a revelation for na young me. They asked why I was dressed like that because I had let myself go.

I was not my usual well-dressed self. I explained I had stopped working that I lost all desire to and so did not have money, my clothes had been in the dry cleaners for months. they paid off every backlog and debt, they really were like Jesus to me. Thank God, he will not leave us Comfortless, God knows our frame that we are dust. Psalm 103:9-13, As a father pitied his children so God feels compassion for us, he knows how frail we are, like the grass here today and gone tomorrow. God's love encompassed me in those lonely months and God spoke to me from his word 2 scriptures that fortified my heart and enabled me to withstand the lies and onslaught of the devil through this Man of God called Husband to be.

If we that are evil know how to give good things to our children how much more will He our heavenly father. If they ask for bread he won't give a stone. so why did I think he would give me what I don t like or want (Mathew 7:11) I am your shield and exceeding great reward. (Gen 15:1) Meaning he protects me from anything and would not let anyone hurt me and he compensates me with good. So, when John came calling again as he had been doing I told him off well and asked him to go call all his fire and brimstone and that I never want to see him again. I was very quick to also let him Know that God will not let him or anyone hurt me that God still loves me after all.

This is one of the life lessons I learnt. People blame the devil but what we really refer to as the Devil most times are our personal demons, bad and wrong habits we fail to deal with, deceptions, selfishness, greed, avarice etc. Don t let people fool us with that. Like Pastor John. This was how I was restored back to fellowship with God and to church. This brought to me a realization of the true forgiving nature of God, the true miracle of what it is to be forgiven in the eyes of God. This made a fundamental change in my life, that I felt closer to the Lord than I had ever been as I had experienced something that profound.

Whilst others may have judged me and felt that I would have deserved to have died God had said no, you will live, you are not done yet with this world there is still much to do. I realize that everyone has a secret, a story, that they keep to them- selves, but that God knows all our secrets whether we choose to tell him or not. I call God the keeper of my secret and that he kept this for me with his banner of love.

I knew however from that moment on I had handed my life over to him, to do with as he would, to guide me in my life that I might be the person that he wanted me to be. I continued in the Church, I became a choir coordinator, I was amazed that I was allowed despite what darkness I was holding inside me. I felt like I was fake, I felt that I was unworthy of what I was doing, I was trying so hard to be a good person yet with each success that I attained I could feel that scratching inside me, like a weight inside my soul.

That if the others in the Church should ever find out what I had done as a believing Christian that I would be removed from the Church, outcast, yet I told no one for fear that I would not be able to serve God. Every day I prayed to God thanking him for his blessing of sparing my life and praying that he would guide me to make me worthy of his love again. As for John I will tell you what happened to him later in this book.

I HAVE DONE A VERY BAD THING

4. I HAVE DONE A VERY BADTHING

The choir rehearsal was going on great as usual we were getting ready for Sunday Service. As we rounded up rehearsals, one of the young girls in the choir asked to speak with me. I had no idea what it was that she wanted to talk to me about but I followed her out- side. She turned to me and threw herself into my arms, she cried and clung to me, weeping so hard, all I could think was that someone she loved had died, that some- thing desperately bad had happened to her. I held her in my arms as she cried, I could almost feel her pain inside with my own, all I wanted to do was to help her, to know what had made her feel this pain so deeply.

She looked up at me with swollen eyes and said to me, "I have done a terrible thing, I have done a terrible thing". From the look in her eyes, I knew what she was going to say before she said it, I could recognize the same pain in her eyes, I could see myself. I had to ask her, she said, I have had an abortion. To have it confirmed, to hear those words, I didn't need to speak, I could feel what she was feeling, her pain was my pain, I just held her so tight, it was like I couldn't hold her close enough to me. I wanted so much to take away her pain, to let her know that she was not alone, to take away her pain, her shame, her guilt, to let her know that God still loved her and knew her pain and could for- give, I felt like my heart was going to break. As I held her in my arms I could feel the tears welling up inside me, we both cried and cried. There was no need for words, I under- stood, I was so shocked and honoured that she felt she could trust me with such a secret, with her pain, her vulnerability, I was the choir coordinator, there was such a risk for

For as the heavens are far from the earth so are his thoughts from our thoughts. He is the magnanimous and ever loving God. Always embracing never forsaking.

her to tell me. Yet, she did this, the only words that I could bring to her pain were that of a hymn which I sang to her softly as we both cried and held her in my arms. I was trying to tell her that yes this is bad but, that God loves you and that God s plan for you, for your life cannot be truncated by this. Yes, this is a terrible thing but, that God s love and mercy is endless and is not defined by the will or opinion of others, there is restoration with God and a new life with him. I developed a close relationship with her from that but never once brought up the subject again. I then began to think, just how many young girls in church are going through something like this?

If they are would they even want to talk about it? So, made up my mind to be especially caring of the young ladies in my care or that I come across to make my self-approachable and to speak to them at their level not Christianise but real life real conversations. I have since met a few young ladies who have even done worse and at the point of giving up on God altogether they confided in me. I remember another sister who had done like 3 different abortions for a minister in Church and she confided in me why? I think there is something about being broken in God's hands, it allows Gods aroma of love seep through the broken cracks and perhaps attract other broken vessels to that sweet savour of His saving grace.

I may not have the perfect explanation for it but since then young ladies have always been able to approach me and I have also purposed not to be judgmental of anyone. We all are products of grace I won't divulge any other details on these girls, suffice to say that in God s mercy and love and by his will they are married. This is a marriage that people dream about and they have children through the grace of God, because they gave themselves over to God and he guided them to become the people that He needed them to be.

I feel that God brought me to them, to help save them, to show them his love and forgiveness, that this is not the end of life and that no one is damned for terrible decisions that they have made. God is a God of a second chance, a third chance and so forth. God does not judge the way man does for He says that His ways are not our ways nor His thoughts our thoughts. For as the heavens are far from the earth so are his thoughts from our thoughts. He is the magnanimous and ever loving God. Always embracing never forsaking.

I MEET MY LOVE

5. I MEET MY LOVE

I was scheduled to sing at a wedding ceremony one day when one of the choir members introduced to me, a young man said to be a very talented gospel musician. He was tall dark and handsome. He then asked me if he could come by the church office to see me. He said they were starting a new branch of their church in Nigeria. I asked him what church it was and when he mentioned the name Bishop Duncan Williams, I was immediately eager to assist them. Bishop was a very good friend of our Senior pastor and someone I closely followed. I had also picked up intercession as one of the ministries to serve in and Bishop Duncan Williams was an Apostle of prayer, so I was more than happy to help the new church start up. When he came by the office the first thing I noticed about him was the way he talked. He was very charming and not churchy at all. He told me how pretty I looked and how glad he was that was helping them. He then would use endearments like Sweetheart and stuff and I remember telling him off very sternly and warning him not to call me by any sweet name or pet name because I have not given him the permission to do so.

I was not having any foolishness or hanky-panky. I was Miss Holi- ness now and did not want any sinner or pretender to make me sin. You see my encounter with John had left me somewhat scarred and I was very shy of men. I did not want any attention from the opposite sex. In short I was married to Jesus, period. Well this young man was not fazed at all. He very politely apologized and thanked me for helping them with sound tracks and some worship songs to use in their new church. We then parted ways.

> Well it was obvious I could not get him to stop calling me all these things. Can you imagine, I was busy minding my business doing Gods business when God sent me my own husband.

I was invited one day by my friends who were members of a gospel group Jesus Messengers. They were to sing at a crusade and asked me to help with additional songs of praise in Yoruba (They were formerly based in Delta state and not very conversant with Yoruba songs). Having a rich repertoire as the worship leader of one of the biggest churches in Lagos then, it was not uncommon to be asked to help every now and then by churches or just gospel musicians. After rehearsal, they invited me to go with them to the crusade. I was not singing with them so I just went along for the experience.

On getting there their drummer a very good friend of mine called Biodun, ran up to me and said, there is someone here who is eager to speak to you. He asked me to invite you over to the stage to seat with us. I followed only to see this   annoying   man again, the one that calls me sweetheart darling, Baby. Imagine. I could not go back because it was over crowded and to get another seat in that crowd was going to be difficult so I reluctantly sat with this annoying man. He kept staring and smiling sheepishly. The next thing he said was "I FEEL LIKE AM STANDING NEXT TO MY WIFE", to which I replied oh where is she, can you introduce us? of course I knew what he was implying but remember I was already very angry to see him. He laughed and said you are the one I am talking about. I completely ignored him as best I could, until they called him out to sing.

I DID A VERY BAD THING

As soon as he sang his first note, the whole atmosphere changed, there was a shift in the spirit, literally the anointing fell. I forgot that I was annoyed I was caught up in this wonderful presence that was evoked. I mean people were worshipping, crying, praying and he was belting out the song with such grace and glory. He seemed like one of the most gifted singers I believe in all of Africa if not worldwide. I was stunned. Wow this worldly brother, who has not quoted any scriptures at me, or prayed fervently in strange very spiritual tongues before taking the microphone but who rather was just a regular young man morphed into this super anointed vessel of God. Then I noticed for the first time how all the girls were thronging him, yet he only had eyes for me. By the way that is what he said when I called his attention to how all the girls seemed to want his attention, his reply was, I only have eyes for you sweetheart.

Well it was obvious I could not get him to stop calling me all those things. Can you imagine, I was busy minding my business doing Gods business when God sent me my own husband. I did not have to stress or fight for it was the Lords doing and beautiful in our sight. That was how we became friends at least. Then he would visit me always in the company of Abiodun and then he would buy me little gifts here and there. He would write poems and songs, and send his friend Abiodun to tell me how much he really liked me and if I would please go on a date with him. It was not over-spiritual thing, there was no "God told me you are my wife" business, it was honest and straight forward, he made his intentions clear from the beginning and befriended me.

We would go out and attend concerts events. He started teaching me how to play the key board and asked me to teach him the art of worship or worship as a ministry. He was a professional musician well-schooled and he could play about 4 or 5 musical instruments, while I was a worship leader/teacher of the word, training new believers and raising worship leaders for our different church branches. After a while, asked him to let us seek Gods face concerning 'us'. We went on a fast and separately waited on God in prayer. After this I introduced him to my Pastor and he introduced me to his pastor. They then asked us to go and pray some more and we did. We both came back and we were persuaded that this was what we wanted. I don t know maybe because of my previous experience with John, I was somewhat not too keen on too many spiritual exercises I was simply weary.

For the first time as a Christian I experienced romance love in the lord, no pressure or force but beautiful wooing, He would sing to me on the streets literally and serenade me for hours, I would be so embarrassed sometimes because he would be singing at the top of his voice on Lagos streets. I introduced him to my family and they all loved him. He was a perfect gentleman, the kind that opened doors for a lady, would stand up when you come to table and help you out of your chair. If he travelled out he usually comes back with little tokens like Teddy Bears. It was like God was comforting me for my painful past.

The next thing he said was "I FEEL LIKE AM STANDING NEXT TO MY WIFE", to which I replied eh where is she, can you introduce us?

This was not usual practice among most African young men, especially the church ones. His parents were both medical Doctors and his siblings were mostly living in the United States of America. He was like an adopted son of Bishop Duncan Williams. I felt safe because Bishop was a man of integrity. We did not court for too long and by the grace of God, we were married. It was beautiful, love, happiness, caring everything that I had hoped for in a relationship, I had never been so grateful for what I had received as we started our new life together in our first year, we needed to establish our own relationship first. This isn't unusual for any new young couple together yet there was a part of me that could feel that scratching at the back of my head getting louder.

The first year passed and we started to plan for a family, the second year passed and still we were not able to have a successful pregnancy. By the third year, people would come to me and ask when they would hear the sound of little feet, I could feel the shame inside me scratching away at my soul. I believed that this was my punishment, that God was punishing me for my sin, so that I would realize the depth of what I had done. Both my husband and I went to the doc- tor, the doctor said that there was something wrong with my tubes inside. I don t know if this was because of the abortion, that something had gone wrong or had not been done properly. I had treatment which allowed me to get pregnant. I remember the first time that I found out that I had conceived, I was so happy and would pray to God that I would be a good enough mother to my child. After about four months, after I had cleared the first trimester, which I know is meant to be the most delicate time of pregnancy, I would lose the child.

Seeing the blood again brought back the memories of the abortion, the pain, the fear, shame, guilt, the scratching in my mind. I felt that God is trying to tell me something, that maybe this was to remind me that I must work harder to be a better mother to be worthy of the gift of life. Time passed and I became pregnant again, again after the first trimester I would lose the child. I cannot tell you of the torture of this, the feeling that I was being punished for my sin, my husband shared this pain. I could understand the punishment that I was receiving but the guilt and pain that I felt for my husband was overwhelming, that he should also have to suffer for my sin. I would pray to God, to show me the way, to show what I must do to be redeem myself. My church would pray for me for us, I still told no one of my past, I would cry every night, I was so aware of everyone trying to help me whilst inside if felt like not only my child had died but that I was also dying.

I could not hold my head up in church, the weight of my past hung around my neck like a millstone, I was so scared that this would be my penance for ever. Everyone could put their blessings on me, they were so kind but I felt so unworthy of their love, of my husband's love. Of feeling that I was not worthy to carry his child and the shame of the pain that I was bringing to him because of my past. Because what I had done was now haunting not only my life but those around me, I wanted it to end so much. Again, I felt so alone, so isolated in my secret pain and the fear of people finding out what I had done, the fear of them saying to me that I deserved it, because there was part of me that felt I did. My secret, that scratched away inside me was so loud and I tried so hard to keep it quiet, I prayed to God, the keeper of my secret for guidance.

> That I had not allowed my faith in God to heal me, but now I had reached the end of that journey, now I realized what I needed to do was to honestly give over to God and understand that I do not have the control over my body or over my future as much as I wanted to.

Eventually after a while, everything came to a head. I was with my husband, we were making love, holding each other in a loving embrace. I wanted to so much to please him, to share in his love and be close to him to his pain and mine. I looked up at him and he looked deep into my eyes and he paused, I could see the pain in his eyes as they welled up and he broke down into tears. I held him as I could feel his pain inside him, he had tried so hard to be strong for both of us, every time we had lost a child. I wanted so much to believe that there was something else that had happened that had upset him, I wanted it to be something else, something that had caused this. I knew, I know that I knew what was causing his pain, I reached inside myself to gather the courage to ask him what was wrong. He could barely look at me, as he sobbed he told me that he felt that he was a failure, that my miscarriages were his fault.

His words cut me so deeply, so far inside, I felt like the breath had been sucked out from my lungs, like my skin had turned cold. How could I tell him? How could I say to him that it was not his fault, that the blame lay solely with me, with my guilt, my shame from a decision that I had made many years before. I cried with him, but we were crying for different reasons, we held each other. I prayed to God, I said that if this is punishment for what I have done, then it is just and I cannot fault you, but your Word says that you are merciful, please God, have mercy on me.

The words I spoke were true and honest and with all my heart as I knelt before God. My mother in-law called us, she spoke about Billings method of conception, this is where you monitor your periods so you can tell when you ovulate. I listened to her and thought to myself, 'I don t have regular periods so how can I tell when I will be able to conceive by this when I can't predict when they will start'? I remember sitting on the edge of the bath looking at this chart, with all the unfamiliar science about how long a male's sperm is meant to live, times of ovulation and conception windows. I just looked up to the Lord and said, God, you are the creator, I believe that if you choose you can make a sperm live for as long as you wish it. I put down the papers, I was so sick and tired of the medical procedures, the medications, and the internal investigations that I had gone through.

The clinical and intrusive examinations which made me feel like the same piece of meat that I had experienced before the years before, each one promising to heal me, clinging to each chance to rectify the sin I had made so many years before but each time failing. I put my hand up to the Lord and said, God, if you heal me, then I will be healed, if you save me, then I will be saved. I had reached a point where I felt that I had stopped running from God, I think that I had been hiding behind the medicines and sciences in the hope that they could heal me and put my faith in man instead of God. That I had not allowed my faith in God to heal me, but now I had reached the end of that journey, now I realized what I needed to do was to honestly give over to God and understand that I do not have the control over my body or over my future as much as I wanted to.

That I had to trust in the will of God rather than man, so rather than continuing to push and push to have a child by any means necessary, I forgot about it, I carried on with my husband the way that we always had and decided that if the Lord will sit I will have a child, if he doesn't then I must accept that.

A MOTHER AT LAST

6. A MOTHER AT LAST

> My shocked changed to excitement, I was so happy, I could feel the thrill flush through me, I had goose bumps all over my skin, my heart started racing.

Three months passed and my husband told me that I was pregnant. I didn't believe him, I didn't t even consider it, I had stopped counting, my periods were irregular so I paid no mind to it. I was in Church and so many were saying that I was pregnant, I would laugh and say that everyone is trying to be prophetic, trying to say that I am pregnant and I'm not. I would tell them to get on with the sermon so that we could hear the word of God rather than these ideas of nonsense.

As time passed I noticed that my skirts and clothes were not fitting but I thought that I was simply putting on some weight. I started to feel unwell so I went to the doctor, he had been a specialist gynaecologist for over twenty years. He told me that I was pregnant, I was so sure that I wasn't I just said I'm not pregnant. Everyone was praying for my pregnancy, the gynaecologist was telling me I was pregnant, my husband was telling me that I was pregnant and I wouldn't believe it. I have no idea what God was thinking when he was looking down on me with my attitude while all this was going on around me. The doctor looked at me confident in his assessment and said okay if you are so sure then we shall do a scan, I was so sure he was wrong but I agreed. I remember sitting down on the bed as the nurse rolled up my shirt and put the cold gel over my stomach and pressed the sensor into my skin.

She turned the monitor to me and pointed, I looked and I will never forget the shock that reached inside me and grabbed hold of my heart. I saw the baby. My shocked changed to excitement, I was so happy, I could feel the thrill flush through me, I had goose bumps all over my skin, my heart started racing. Hope filled me like a summer sun warming me from the outside in, I thought could this be the one? As soon as I stepped outside of the hospital, pain hit me, I started bleeding, I bent over in agony as the contractions gripped me like a vice inside. I tried pulling myself together because that very same day there was a special service, a wedding where I was officiating with the choir. I put on a sanitary towel and told myself that it was nothing, but that did not stop the panic from filling me, it did not stop the tears from gushing down my face like a waterfall. All that kept going through my mind was 'not again please God not again, I can't cope with this Lord, I am not strong enough please', I begged and prayed.

When I got to the Church I rushed to the changing room. I was in agony, doubled over in pain and fear, I called to my husband to come to me, I was so scared. He asked me what was wrong and what had happened, he was obviously very concerned. I told him that I had seen the baby, he was so happy and couldn't understand why I was so upset. The shame and fear gripped me, I tried so hard to find the words to tell him, I had so little strength inside me and felt so weak. I didn't want the pain for either of us. I had to tell him, I was bleeding again, that I was so scared that I was going to lose the baby, that I was there to officiate a wedding that I didn't feel that I could go on. He said to me, "So, what is happening? Do you want to sing or you don t want to sing?" I stopped dead in shock at hearing these words, I couldn't believe the coldness of his response.

"So, you not even going to hold me or tell me" he cut me off in my words. He said listen, "God has done this, he has given you a child, are you going to believe in God, or are you going to believe the signs you're seeing? If God wills that you are going to have this child then believe God". I was shocked, I had no idea that he could be so cold but I look back on this now and I think that he must have been also going through the pain and the shame of losing so many children so many times. I was so lost in my world that I could not connect to him, I could not appreciate the pain that he was also going through at that time. He said, "if you want to believe God, then come out and sing", and he walked out of the room.

The wedding was from one of my church sisters who was marrying one of the church brothers, they were both very popular in the Church and there were many guests. I sat there in the changing room, hearing the business of the other guests as I contemplated my options. It was a test of faith for me, do I believe in God s will that I should have this child, or do I believe that I will lose this child like I have every other before it. Do I believe God or do I believe the glaring evidence? The answer came to me that if you believe in the Lord your God, then he will bless your bread and your water, he will take sickness away from your midst, and the number of your days he will fulfil, none shall abort, none shall miscarry. That day, I took those words and in such pain, fever and sickness, I got up and walked out, holding back the tears in my eyes and walked to the pulpit to join my choir. I stood there with the pain of my body that I might cure my soul and I sang.

I DID A VERY BAD THING

I sang to the Lord to worship him, to praise him, for his Word is stronger and mightier that the flesh of man. With the Lord in my heart I was signing, I was dancing, I was telling people that if they cannot dance just sway the Lord will know what is in your heart. I could feel myself bleeding, I could feel the pain, the contractions as I was with the choir. For four hours, I danced and sang to the Lord in worship of the unison of this young couple's wedding and I praised God. I thought to myself that if God will save me then he will save me, if he will not save me then let it be on this alter here that this child will fall. I thought this because at that point I did not qualify to be a mother, the thought was now solid in my mind, as I sang I could feel the tears flowing down my face and the pain gripped tight inside of me. I reached inside my heart and remembered those words of God that his mercy heals all, so I stood there and saw it to the end.

I had to tell him, I was bleeding again, that I was so scared that I was going to lose the baby, that I was there to officiate a wedding that I didn't feel that I could go on.

The mercy of the Lord is vast and unending, for God saw fit that day to grant me a child, my son and not only did I have that baby, but the Lord saw that I was a fit mother and chose to bless me with a second. Each year in Church, they have a celebration on mothering Sunday for all those blessed with children. They have a cup which they give to them, each time, I know that I did not qualify for it, so I am so humble and grateful for what I have, so much more given what had happened before. I am reminded that God does not judge us by our mistakes, he does not hang it over our head, that is something that we do to ourselves.

We must believe, know and have faith that God will forgive us, because we cannot forgive ourselves or each other at times. It isn't God that punishes us, we punish ourselves because that we feel that we deserve it. I felt that I deserved every loss, that God was angry with me for my sin, oh but he wasn't, I was. It wasn't until that day that I was able to realize this, that my belief that I deserved what had happened to me needed to be punished that I tortured myself and ignored what gifts that God was trying to give to me. But that day, I gave up my own will to accept God s blessing, to accept the gift of life that he was trying to bestow on me and I took it with both arms so tightly. It was through the love and acceptance of God that I could learn to love and accept myself again through that child, that blessing.

WHAT BECAME OF JOHN?

7. WHAT BECAME OF JOHN?

A few years after I broke up with   John   just before I met my husband, I was asked by our Senior pastor to go along with him to a crusade of sorts. This was normal because my Pastor usually takes me along on his outreaches, especially crusades and major speaking events. He would ask that I do a song or 2 or maybe just minister in songs as led by the Holy Spirit, that one is a talk for another day. He does not pick songs for me nor does he even tell me what he is speaking on most times, except if maybe there is a Theme for the event we are going for.

He would usually say something like, "If you are intoned with the Holy Spirit you will sing a song in season and I am not making this up, it was that kind of training so I had to be on top of my game as a worship leader or music minister, always holding tight to the Holy Spirit and keeping my inner ears open to hear what song to do. Thank God who is rich in mercy that He always gave me a song in season. And we would see God move in wonderful ways.

Then came in her husband who is the host minister who had invited my pastor to this crusade and I almost jumped out of my skin. Lo and be-hold it was John. Yikes!!

There are times that I would be asked to take a team with me and other times I would be asked to come alone, so I would take along sound tracks or just prepare a song to do with the music team in the host church or event. However, on this day, My Pastor asked that I come with a team, and he also had quite an entourage that goes with him. So, all of us (about 10 people) were attending this crusade in Ajegune Lagos state.

When we arrived, we saw the stage that had been erected outside, but there was darkness everywhere, no electricity for the light bulbs or to power the music instruments. There were some few people gathered and some sort of singing was going on. I thought to myself whoever this pastor is or minister that invited our pastor is going to get an ear full, cause if you live in Nigeria then, and was organizing an event the first thing you ensure is power supply be- cause electricity supply was erratic or sporadic at best. I was already feeling sorry for whoever the host was. We were then ushered into this room in the house and a woman rushed in bringing food, like rice, hot sodas and frantically trying to attend to us. There were 2 little children nearby, obviously, her kids and she was trying her best to handle the situation. Then came in her husband who is the host minister who had invited my pastor to this crusade and I almost jumped out of my skin. Lo and behold it was John, Yikes!!

I cannot begin to explain what kind of thoughts were jumping around in my head or the emotions that accompanied them. Lord have mercy! I felt shock, then sorrow for them, being in this pathetic situation, even the fliers they came to show us was black and white, honestly it was such a pitiable situation. Then I felt this all-consuming Joy!! Because this could have been me!!I could have been the woman sweating profusely, balancing one baby in hand and a toddler tagging along while trying to serve food for important guests at my husband's crusade. I don t know if we spoke to each there because my pastor just called him aside to discuss quietly and soon we were out the door, back in the church vehicles and driving away. It was a very pathetic situation, with no working microphones for an obviously ill prepared 3-day crusade, a broken-down generator which some repair man was unsuccessfully attempting to fix? My people, we did not return for the crusade!

Fear would not even let me ask my Pastor anything, I just went on my knees thanking God for his awesomeness, God in his infinite mercy helped me dodge a deadly bullet. I mean I was so terrified at what I could have become. I wondered for years what became of them. Two years ago, I got a visit from a friend and sister who was among the people that were so mad at me for not marrying   the man of God and she told me an even sorrier story. She said she saw John and she could hardly make him up, because he had this huge gash across his face, it was badly stitched and gave him a gory look. She was so stunned and asked him what happened. He explained that he got in fight with a Mallam (people from the Northern part of Nigeria the Hausa speaking ones who did menial jobs around town running corner shops).

Anyway, she told that he said they got in a brawl and the Mallam cut him with his small axe. My goodness this is like 24 years after and I get this information. Now the bible commands us not to joy over even the down fall of our perceived enemy for this is not pleasing to God. So, I don t rejoice over all these things rather I am humbled and thankful that God delivered me from my ignorance and the consequences of the ignorance would have been life altering. At the same time the wicked will not go unpunished o. Let us not be deceived, what a man sows he will reap, except you repent of your sins and ask God s forgiveness. For with God there is forgiveness of sins and God has promised to not remember them nor hold us accountable for them. Psalm 103:2.

CONCLUSION

8. CONCLUSION

For anyone that chooses to read this, this is my way of saying that there is nothing that you have done that can remove the love of God. He knows what is in your heart, he knows what is in your mind, he will never stop giving you the opportunities to heal yourself even if you can' t. His love and mercy are endless. Even though we are hu- man and imperfect, we cannot judge or anticipate that God will feel for us the same way that we may feel about ourselves, that is what makes him far greater than us. So, you need to embrace your life, what has happened has happened, you cannot change that, but you can change yourself now. You can through accepting the love and the faith of God into your lives and know that there is forgiveness through him.

For so long I carried the shame and the pain of what I had done and it affected my life and the life of those around me. Even though they loved me and cared for me they could not help me. It was only through accept- ing God s mercy that I could forgive myself, I won't lie to you that I don t sometimes remember the pain but now, when I consider my chil- dren s I see what the Lord has done. God has a plan for all of us. We just have to embrace it and al- low God into our lives so that we might be- come the person that he wants us to be. Please know that through Him every dream can and will be realized, every desire can be granted, it is not because we have earned it which is the way we were taught to be- lieve. I have learned that God does not work like this. God will love you and accept you when you are ready to accept him and realize that the only one punishing you is yourself.

As for me I thank God that I saw the light through that wonderful family sought me out all the way from America. God is good and will always be faithful to find us and bring us back home no matter how far we have gone or no matter how bad a thing we have done. As a father has compassion on his children so God has for us, he will not always chide us, He understands our frame, our frailties our short comings, He knows how fragile our minds are and how weak our flesh is. As far as the heavens are from the earth, so far has He re- moved our transgressions from us and He says if our sin be as red as crimson He makes us white again even as wool. (Psalm 103:12-14).

We have a loving Father, committed Lover an everlasting Friend, He won't give up on us even when we are sure we don t qualify He qualifies us, He sends us help even when we are not talking to Him and run away from Him, He is always reaching out to hold us in His embrace and tell us "You are Mine and I won't let you go". Today I have 3 wonderful children. And am still very much in Love with Jesus. My journey in my short life has been interesting, I have been separated from my husband and then widowed, Life Happened to us, but through it all I learnt to trust in Jesus and to Rely on my God (Isaiah 50:10). I have come a long way from being a fledging worship leader, I now am a full-fledged film maker, an actress, Director Producer with multi Awards, but God is not done with me yet. Our lives are un- folding and every day I realize God has a plan, God has a purpose and His plan is good and not evil to give us a future and a hope. Yes, I did a very bad thing but God is a very good God.

Nuggets
a) A broken engagement is better than a broken marriage.
b) God loves us unconditionally no matter what we do, we can always return to God.

SUMMARY

9. SUMMARY

I hope that from my story, I may have somewhat encouraged and strengthened you. Especially those of us from a very religious background. We tend to be caught in the vice of 'Spiritual, Religious Bullies', opportunists and even frauds, who come in the Name of the Lord. We need to first of all have a personal world view or belief system, a personal set of convictions that stems from our own deep persuasions separate from what a church or mosque has taught. I learnt from my Mentor that because we do not have our own deep rooted belief system, fully persuaded from our conscience of a universal law of good from evil, we can be easily confused and brain- washed . An example he gave was of a clergyman who at the point of entry to the western world, coming in from Africa, was asked a certain question, he responded and said he was telling the truth and could not lie because he was a pastor.

The immigration officer in amazement and very puzzled asked, if one was not a pastor was it then okay to lie? You see many times we do things based on a set of beliefs that we were taught, we have not taken time for ourselves to develop our own belief system. I was led on a very dark road because I was naive and gullible, I later discovered that what the general people accepted as Kosher was in effect a lie. Now I know God for myself and understand that irrespective of faith, religion or whatever, good is good and evil is evil. I pray that this book will set you free and grant you the courage to speak out against oppression, deception and false teachings. May our light so shine before men, setting them free as we expose all forms of darkness.

ABOUT THE AUTHOR

TOYIN MOORE

Toyin is an Ace Broadcaster and Film Maker whose career currently spans well over a decade, majoring in Television and Film Production, Promoter and Event Convener. Toyin is also a much-sought after motivational speaker with a passionate and very emboldened approach to speaking out about real life issues. Toyin driven passion is to empower women especially those from disadvantaged background. Believes that our responsibility to our environment and ourselves demand that as we all are unique and special we must look closer and develop our God given talents to use for the benefit of mankind.

Some of her works in Film and television include but are not limited to; CHAMPIONS a Drama and Talk Show Program syndicated on several TV Stations in Nigeria and sub Saharan Africa. (2003-2005) -celebrating and profiling ordinary people doing extra ordinary things a grace to grass stories, encouraging diligence hard work and never give up spirit. TUMINIS SONG. (Producer). (2005). PATRICK 1 & 2 (2005). AT HOME ABROAD TV SERIES 2013 (UK). BLOODTYPE 2014, CAPTIVATED 2015 and several others.

She is currently in production of a very controversial television series APOSTLE DO GOOD. This addresses the recent happenings with church, clergy and pew. She is also recently started a Live Video Broadcast on Facebook TY S DIARIES.

This fast becoming one of the most watched broadcast on social media as it discusses most perceived taboo sub- jects with a sincere and open manner so that people are encouraged be transparent and heal.

Toyin is a Multi Award Winner, taking home several Awards, which include the Best Actress, Best Producer, Best Director categories. Toyin is currently residing in the UK with her family.

Social Contacts:

LINKEDIN . Toyin Moore

INSTAGRAM: toyinmoore

FACEBOOK: Toyin Moore

TWITTER: @mooretoyin

VIDEOGRAPHY